Peace and Freedom

Loden Nyima

Published by Loden Nyima, 2024.

While every precaution has been taken in the preparation of this book, the publisher assumes no responsibility for errors or omissions, or for damages resulting from the use of the information contained herein.

PEACE AND FREEDOM

First edition. February 19, 2024.

ISBN: 979-8224783342

Written by Loden Nyima.

Table of Contents

Introduction

Meditation is a healthy and natural activity that absolutely everyone can do.

For some, it's a vital part of wellness, rejuvenation, and strength, and may not necessarily include a spiritual path. For others, it's foundational and central to Buddhist practice. Or, meditation may play a role in any number or combination of different spiritual or religious paths.

All of this is very warmly welcome.

My intention in writing and teaching meditation is to offer whatever I can to help, wherever that leads you, with no strings attached. Not only do I really mean that, but it's tremendously inspiring to me to practice with people from many interests and walks of life. Being blessed to lead many retreats to that effect with all kinds of amazing people is what inspired this book.

It has three sections. The first, "Introduction to Meditation Practice" starts from square one with how to meditate. The second, "Journeying into Shamatha" goes farther into teachings on the development of shamatha, or peaceful abiding meditation. It includes the general road map of how our practice progresses, what we tend to work with as it does, and making peace with ourselves and resting at deeper levels. The third, "Vipashyana and the Four Foundations of Mindfulness" is about freeing our minds through insight.

It's short and to the point to the best of my limited abilities. It was intended to support meditation practice itself, and to be easily read during the weekend retreats I often lead, to be used at home as a resource and inspiration, for all my friends teaching meditation, and for anyone interested in learning.

There are a few things that are traditionally said when beginning teachings, and the longer I've taught, the more true I've realized them to be: It's all been said before much better than I will here. I bow to my own teacher Shakyamuni Buddha, to everyone who conveyed his teachings to me, and to the innate wisdom within everyone who will read this. May what little I've been able to understand and convey be of benefit. Any faults are my purely my own.

Section One: Introduction to Meditation Practice

How to Meditate

Meditation is a process of trusting ourselves and coming home.

We often come to meditation for relief from stress, turmoil, or from inspiration for meaning and truth. It's that very part of ourselves seeking such things that already has them. It's *like* longing for *like*. It's our innate wisdom, compassion, and freedom shining through. We're learning to trust that intuitive part of ourselves, to come home, and let it expand.

Shamatha is a Sanskrit word that means "peaceful abiding." It describes an ancient form of meditation that predates Buddhism by a long shot and has been practiced by people of many or no religious traditions for thousands of years. Many of the teachings we know today in the popular mindfulness movement were derived from these and related teachings, either from Buddhism, Yoga, or other traditions.

Anyone can practice shamatha, we don't need to have any interest in Buddhism. And if we *do* have an interest in Buddhism, shamatha is foundational to our meditation practice and is something we'll use extensively.

While it's called "peaceful abiding," I would say that in shamatha we make peace with ourselves, and as a result, we're able to rest. The struggle is over, and the natural stability, clarity, and strength of our mind and heart can be as they are. I'll take us through how to do this.

The first step is to find a posture that allows for the length from our seat through the torso to the crown of our head to be upright, open, and relaxed without tension or pain. This is commonly done sitting on a meditation cushion with our legs crossed, ensuring that our seat is positioned high enough so that our knees are lower than our hips. Sitting on a chair can work equally well, ideally with our feet grounded and flat on the floor and our back upright, not leaning against the back of the chair.

Sometimes we have to experiment with smaller support cushions, folded blankets, or the like, to help find a posture that works for us. We can rest our hands on our thighs or folded in our laps. We can also meditate lying down flat on our backs, or even standing up. Our eyes usually remain open but resting gently on the floor in front of us. The idea is that we don't need to escape in order to find peace.

Next, we become aware of our breathing. We really feel our breathing. We've been doing it our whole lives, but how does it feel to breathe? How does it feel for the breath to come through our bodies and back out into space? We *become our breathing.*

Within the feeling of our body breathing, we allow ourselves to feel whatever we feel. We might feel pain, pleasure, tiredness, alertness, lingering emotional energy from our day—whatever it is, it's welcome. We welcome it into our breath.

The attitude here is one of complete friendliness to ourselves, total acceptance. Sometimes we think meditation is about finding some separate peace away from our problems, but real peace is the peace we make with ourselves. It's the peace that comes from being willing to feel whatever we feel, and breathe, and rest as we are.

So this is basically it, we sit and we breathe.

It's deceptively simple, because what we're doing is actually extremely profound. We're learning that we have and are everything we need, just as we are, and can sit down and rest. We can deepen, open, and grow, and from that, we engage in the world.

As we continue to sit and breathe, we'll also begin to notice all the activity in our minds and find ourselves distracted in thoughts. Each time we notice this, we simply and very gently return to our breath. We're learning that we can notice our thoughts and return to the breath, that we don't have to be trapped in a prison of our own making, trapped by believing everything we think. We can breathe.

We'll also experience emotional energy, strong feelings, unprocessed material, and so on. We'll talk more about that in one of the next chapters called "Our Self-Healing, Self-Rejuvenating Mind." But the pith is, instead of getting caught up in the stories and narratives we have about these emotions, we find the raw feeling or energy in our body and hold it, breathe with it, love it, like massaging a knot in a muscle—in this case, with our breathing.

Meditation is something we can do a few minutes a day, three breaths at a time at any moment, or for years in retreat. The right amount is the amount that feels attainable and inspiring for us. Gradually, we're stabilizing, clarifying, and strengthening our minds and hearts, or rather, letting those natural qualities grow. It can definitely have a lot of benefits, but we'll have to see for ourselves how it works for us and trust our experience.

Becoming Our Own Best Friend

All of us long for connection. It's just part of what we are. From a Buddhist point of view, it's actually a form of our innate compassion, even if it's all tangled up into loneliness or grasping at others to make us feel at ease. The irony is, we're connected already…but more on that in a bit.

We all want friends to talk to, people to share life with, to enjoy the ups and support the downs, people to understand us, to love us. To a greater or lesser extent, we want to offer that to others, in one big cycle. And that's a wonderful thing!

And, we're the only ones who can give that to ourselves completely. The more we offer unconditional love to ourselves, the more loving and healthy our relationships with others will be. The more we have to give, the more our innate compassion unfolds and embraces others. The more that happens, the more we feel how much of that also comes our way.

We are the only ones who are with ourselves constantly, through every single moment of our life, and even our death.

So, why not make friends with ourselves?

We can do this by accepting ourselves completely, exactly the way we are. We can give ourselves unconditional love and support by being willing to feel exactly what we feel. We can breathe with it all, remaining, being, trusting, loving. This is what we do in meditation.

Whether what we experience is pleasurable, painful, insightful, or confusing, the whole mix—whatever comes our way—we can feel it all. We don't have to be trapped in our inner monologues like a prison of our own thoughts. We can be with our breathing, feel our breathing, become our breathing. We're naturally present, naturally connected, naturally feeling beings. We can just feel, breathe, allow, and be. This is a profound form of listening.

As we do, we are likely to encounter periods of rest and relief, and periods of more emotional upheaval. We may even encounter trying very hard to meditate properly and judging ourselves harshly if we feel like we're not.

The idea is to feel and *allow it all* with softness, friendliness, acceptance, and trust; to just invite it into our breathing, into our body breathing. When we give ourselves and those experiences lots of warmth and space, it's like holding and soothing an upset child or pet—like that, but with ourselves, with our breathing. And, if we find we're being "hard on ourselves," then we can be "soft about being hard on ourselves"—-in other words, we can hold that too, just as it is. Everything, everything, everything, is allowed, invited, and included.

This is the practice of making friends with ourselves.

The more we do this, the more we can come home to our natural contentment, peace, and well-being. And, the more that our capacity to feel our connectivity, our compassion, can unfold and embrace others, eventually, everyone and everything.

We've never actually been separate, we've never been isolated. We're made of the elements of the earth, as is everything and everyone we encounter on a daily basis. We're made from our parents, shaped by our experiences, sustained by the work of others, sustaining others with ours. Loving, hating, being loved, being hated—it's all in connection with others.

We've never been alone. We've just been trapped. And we can be free.

Freedom from the Inner Netflix

First of all, I actually love Netlflix, so if anyone from there reads this, please don't sue me or cancel my subscription—my problem isn't with you!

This chapter is about what I call, the "inner Netflix"—-the repetitive stories, dramas, and narratives, that play out in our minds over and over again. Like the situation in our life that we think about constantly, whether at the workplace, or in our relationships, or other situations. It's the thing we keep mulling over, "if only I had, if only they had, one day it will be this way, next time I see them I'll say this," and so on. Or, we review the list of things we have to do later, or the big regrets we have, or the endless self-criticism, or the various fantasies, or the hopes and fears and anxieties about the future. The list goes on and on.

The inner Netflix has it all. We've got the drama, the workplace sitcom, the relationship stuff, the family show, maybe some "emo," the revenge fantasies, and the action and adventure. Let's hope there's no crime, and not too much apocalyptic sci-fi beyond the news. Oh, and they're mostly reruns. In Buddhism we call these "habitual patterns." And sorry Netflix, but yeah, that applies to you too.

The issue is, we actually believe it.

Just like on Netflix, the more we get into our shows, the more we feel pleasure and pain, joy and suffering, depending what's going on. Meanwhile, the actors are off doing their thing, they've never been in our apartment or house. It's just been us and our laptop the whole time.

Our minds are like this too.

Our "inner Netflix," the repetitive stories we play out in our minds, have only ever been as solid or real as we've made them by believing them, by replaying them, by giving them our energy. They only have power because we keep subscribing. And often, then we and others act them out in life, and "all the world's a stage"...

Really, our minds are free, open, and connected, like a nice big screen that can display whatever it wants, but isn't stuck in any one show. And really, there is no screen either: it's just space, wisdom, and love...and it's free. It's more like the sky, sun, earth, water, and wind that all our gadgets and shows are made of. No purchase necessary—it's what we are.

In meditation, we learn to notice when we're getting stuck in habitual patterns, let go, and allow them to dissolve. We do this by remaining present with our breathing, nice and easy, natural, and free. When we find ourselves distracted or caught up in our stories, we can just gently return to our breath. In fact, we're already "back," since the awareness that noticed we were caught up in thought was never itself distracted! So we can just relax, trust ourselves, breathe, and let go.

In meditation we're shifting our subscription to our breathing, and ultimately, to our nature—our openness, wisdom, compassion, and freedom. And we can unsubscribe from the rest. It's caused us enough trouble already, and besides, we've seen all the episodes before. Many, many, many times.

Now if you'll excuse me, it's back to *Breaking Ba*—uh, oh, I mean meditation. Yeah, meditation first.

Our Self-Healing, Self-Rejuvenating Mind

Many of us these days come to meditation or a spiritual path with a wish to heal. We want to heal from one or another form of suffering or turmoil that we've experienced; or from the pace, demands, and challenges of modern life. We often come seeking relief, peace, stillness, rejuvenation, wellness, and even freedom from whatever limiting conditions we experience.

The good news is that those qualities are in us already and are doing the seeking and the asking. While we certainly don't need to be a Buddhist, or even interested in Buddhism, to practice many forms of meditation (and I actually mean that!), one name for this part of ourselves is our Buddha nature. It's our innate wisdom, compassion, freedom, health, and strength. The way it shines through in our lives can be by recognizing that we're suffering and that we long to heal, to release, to be free. It's *like* longing for *like*. It's the sun shining through the clouds, present all along.

Whatever we call it, innately, our minds and hearts are wise, compassionate, connected, strong, resilient, and open. Otherwise, how would we have gone through all the ups and downs of life and still be here? Why would we care about other people, the world, or even ourselves or our pets? How would we know how we feel, what feels right and wrong, and what we need to do? Why on earth would we want to meditate?

Like the sky accommodates all kinds of weather, our innate wisdom, compassion, and openness have accommodated everything we've experienced in life.

However, to the extent that we get hung up on various thoughts, emotions, and experiences, or when they simply overwhelm us, or when we get hurt, there's a part of ourselves that gets stuck. It's sort of like a knot in a muscle, or a physical injury that gets stiff. Only, with emotions, it's on a more subtle level, and it creates a sort of knot in our spiritual body, and often even in our physical body.

We all know the saying, "I had a knot in my stomach," or perhaps the feeling of being so shut down that it feels like there's lead in our chest, or we feel so nervous, we have butterflies inside, or tension in our head, or so angry we feel hot, and so on. This is what I'm talking about—there's an almost physical, metastasized quality to our emotions. In Buddhism we explain this through a subtle, spiritual, body that's related to our nervous system, and so much more...

The good news is that we can actually heal and release these things completely. As a matter of fact, our minds and hearts, ourselves, our nature, are actually self-healing, self-rejuvenating, and even self-liberating or freeing! Like the sky...

The way we do this is by feeling what we feel, embracing ourselves totally as we are, and breathing. As we contact strong emotions, we can get *curious about where they actually are in our body*. How do they feel? What are they made of? Where are they?

Like massaging a knot in a muscle, we can gently breathe with our stuck emotions, with total acceptance, warmth, and love. We can trust ourselves enough to do that. As we do, we can remain curious about how our emotions feel and where the space is in them. We can give them that space with our breath. And eventually, they loosen up, they melt, like ice back into water, or clouds dissolving in the sky. Our sky. Everyone's sky.

As this happens, we can rest at deeper and deeper levels, and we can also learn that our thoughts and emotions have only ever been as solid as we've made them. When we embrace them with natural presence, they eventually dissolve, and so do we, and whatever wisdom and connection are within them will only grow. In this way, we can learn to trust our self-healing, self-rejuvenating, self-liberating mind. We can be free.

Coming to Our Senses

The World Meditates Us

All of our senses are an expression of basic wakefulness. Right now, we're seeing, hearing, smelling, tasting, and feeling—because we're awake. And everything we perceive is sacred, living, and free. It's all actually made from the earth and the elements, even if it's so impossibly refined and processed that it's easy to forget that. Isn't the earth sacred?

In meditation, we remember this. Every perception is a reminder, a wake-up call, a notification that we're alive and that life is precious, fleeting, and beautiful. We're part of an ecosystem, a circle of life. This can be an especially helpful way to meditate when we feel scattered, anxious, alone, or stressed out by a situation in our life. It can help us reconnect with our greater whole.

We can do this by grounding our practice in our senses. Let ourselves feel our connection to the earth below us, like a tree with deep roots that go down. The earth has been holding and accommodating us our entire lives; it always will, and it will welcome us home when we die.

Let ourselves hear what we hear, whatever sounds are in our environment. If we can meditate outside, great, but if not, listen not only to the sounds in the room but also to the silence allowing them. Hear the wind, the rain if there is any; we can even hear our heart beating when we settle down.

Let ourselves see what we see. We don't need to escape to meditate. Our eyes can be open and relaxed, down a bit at first, up more once we're settled in. We don't look at anything, yet sights come in, like light coming in through the windows.

Let ourselves feel the warmth all around us, ultimately from the sun, and the warmth within our breathing bodies. Let that warmth melt away any tension we're holding. Let that warmth love us, nourish us, give us life, and invigorate us. Let it hold and melt any stuck emotional energy. Most of our body is made of water. Let it flow, move, connect.

Feel our breathing moving in and out of our body and into our environment. Our breath is our connection with the wind and air all around us. Let our breathing take us beyond ourselves, within ourselves. Let it carry away anything we're holding in our minds as we breathe out. Follow it out into space. Feel it coming back in and flowing through our bodies. Feel it being shared with everyone.

Let ourselves feel what we feel. No right, no wrong. Be who we are. Breathe. Breathe, welcoming with it all. Everything we feel is now. We feel because we're alive. We can feel pleasure, pain, and everything in between. Welcome ourselves home.

Let our minds be like the sky.

Let our thoughts, stories, memories, hopes and fears, dissolve away into it, carried away by the wind of our breath. Don't worry, the wisdom, or intuitive knowing, and compassion within them will only get stronger.

If we'd like, we can do a body scan, gently bringing our awareness to each part of our body, starting with our feet and moving up, taking three breaths with each part, breathing into it, holding any tension with warmth and love, and offering it to the earth, the wind, and the sky. We can know we're made of the elements, whole with the elements, never separate from mother earth, water, fire, wind, space.

If focusing on our body isn't helpful or is even reminiscent of traumatic experiences, instead, we can use whichever of the senses feels grounded and safe to us, like a particular sight in the room, or a sound. We can also place an object we like in front of us and meditate on that. One of my friends uses a pebble from a holy site she visited.

In meditation, we're coming to our senses, and we're *trusting our senses*. Let them do the work! If we relax through our senses, relaxing into what we see, hear, feel, we'll relax into natural wakefulness.

The world meditates us.

If we find ourselves spacing out too much, we can bring our awareness more closely to our breathing. It's up to us to find the appropriate balance between being with our breathing and opening to our senses—and there is no contradiction whatsoever, it's just a matter of how open, big, and free our minds and hearts are ready to be.

Speaking of Silence

Healing in Space and Stillness

When I lead silent meditation retreats, I often begin with a somewhat cynical joke. I ask, "OK, let's have a show of hands, how many people here feel like we can keep up with everything in our lives, process all the information we receive in a day completely, give as much time and care to all of our interactions and relationships as they need, thoughtfully attend to all of our work and tasks with no rush whatsoever, take as much time as we need for self-care and health, relax at the end of the day with not a care in our minds, sleep as much as we need, then wake up the next day refreshed and ready to go?"...At this point, usually we're all chuckling and shaking our heads in empathetic commiseration and the kind of relief that comes from being able to laugh in authentic connection with others.

That said, it's no joke. From a meditative point of view, our spiritual energy, or *pranna,* is part of a subtle body related to our nervous system and more. Every time our mind does something, like taking in information, thinking about things, responding to things—literally any activity whatsoever—our mind and body engage, our *pranna* moves, and we use energy. While I'm a big fan of technology (and am using it now!), it's also my own view that the blazing pace of life and business we're attempting to manage in mainstream U.S.A. simply exceeds what we're physically, emotionally, and spiritually capable of doing in a healthy way.

To put it simply: our technology has outpaced our biology.

For many, this can leave us feeling exhausted, overwhelmed, numb, anxious, depressed, and more. It can make it hard to connect emotionally with ourselves and others, hard to focus, and can even cause physical health issues like insomnia, unexplainable malaise, and more. This is a healthy response to an unhealthy situation, and there's an incredibly helpful, easy, and natural medicine we can offer ourselves: space, silence, and stillness.

Silence—meaning not talking with others, texting, keeping up with apps and news, and so on—has been a support for meditation practice for millennia. As we take in less, do less, we allow ourselves to simply *be.* We can allow our minds and bodies, our *pranna,* to settle and to relax. It's like a detox in a certain way, learning how healthy and natural we actually are.

The next thing I do when I lead silent meditation retreats is to go around in a circle and ask everyone to speak a bit about why they came. Almost universally, there's some desire for healing, rejuvenation, renewal, rest, and depth of spiritual practice. I encourage people to trust exactly that part of ourselves which is seeking those things—-that's our innate wisdom, compassion, sanity, and health shining through! It's our longing to come home, to rest, to return to our true nature. It's *like* longing for *like.*

Our meditation practice itself is a process of coming home. It's a process of embracing ourselves and our experience exactly as we are—being willing to feel whatever we feel, be it pleasure or pain, and to simply breathe and remain present with it all. Meditation is an act of profound friendliness to ourselves, and outrageous acceptance and trust. In the process, we can self-heal and self-rejuvenate whatever unprocessed emotional material is in our minds and bodies, and ultimately learn to rest. Then we can engage in life from that place of well-being, and be all the more available to others.

I've written more about the meditative process in the coming chapters. But for now, silent retreat is a powerful support. It relieves us from keeping up with the pace and demands of life, and lets us settle down and come home to ourselves. It can also amplify whatever is going on in our own minds (because what else is there!?) and, in that way, it can be an extension of the invitation for acceptance, friendliness, feeling, and trust.

I often end silent meditation retreats with another joke. I look around the room at these beaming, lighter, healthier-looking people and say, "you know, you could have done that at home." But what we often don't have at home is each other, and the incredibly moving support and bond that can come from a circle of people sitting together in a supportive place meditating. We've been doing that for thousands of years. Meditation has survived because it works. And of course, we often simply don't have the time and space for that to happen. That's why retreats exist, even if the whole path and result is already within our hearts. Otherwise, why are we reading this?

Daily Practice: Our Reservoir of Sanity

Meditation practice is a lot like physical exercise: the consistency is more important than the amount. Having a daily meditation practice can be key to seeing real benefits in our lives. Every time we practice, it's as if we're deepening our reservoir of sanity, peace, resiliency, from which we can draw at any moment when we need it.

The right amount of daily practice is the amount that feels attainable to us—even on, or *especially on*, a busy day. If we pick an amount that we know we can do, we'll do it, and we'll feel good about it, and that will help us build momentum and want to keep practicing, or even extend our practice.

However, if we pick an amount that's too much, we might get to it once in a while and just feel bad the rest of the time...that doesn't help.

So, err on the easy side. Ten minutes a day can actually be quite good. It sounds small, but try it out and see...or, 15, 20, or 30 minutes, or more, really whatever feels right to you. You're the only one who will know. But start with an amount that's like "oh yeah, I could definitely do that, no problem, in fact I could do more."

Often first thing in the morning can be a good time to practice, or also after work or in the evening. Some people like to do a little bit at each one of those times and build their practice that way. Lunch break can also be a good time. Really whenever you can find in your day that works.

As well, it can be helpful to designate a place in our home or at work that supports our practice. Somewhere we can have our cushion, chair, or whatever we prefer to meditate on. Certainly we want to put our phones away and not have too many things around us that are distracting. We can also arrange any objects that inspire our practice. Outside in nature can also be *perfect*.

Once I was staying with a friend while traveling, and we were drinking coffee in the morning and hanging out. Then, an alarm on his phone went off, and he said "ah, excuse me, it's my time to go meditate." Then he just walked up his stairs, closed his door, and that was that.

I sat there, alone, and went "Woooowwww, he's my HERO!!!"

Then I thought about it, and I thought, you know what, he's got the right idea, that's really what we have to do these days.

The thing is, if we wait for life to slow down in order to practice, we'll die waiting.

Many of us have cultural conditionings that prioritize work, or basically anything others need from us, and *then* if there's time left that's when we take care of ourselves. But really, we're the only ones who get to decide what's meaningful for us in life and how we want to use it. Our boss won't go with us when we die.

The more we practice, the more we care for our own spiritual, emotional, and physical well-being, the more available we are to others and the more helpful we can be to everyone around us. It's an odd kind of selfishness if making time for meditation results in being more patient, kind, loving, and helpful to others. But, we have to start with ourselves, or at least take care of ourselves while we care for others.

An activist I admire greatly once said, "I vow not to burn out."

So, I recommend my friend's method of just putting our meditation time in our phones or on our calendars, and treating it like any other commitment. Then, when life kicks in and there's all kinds of things to do, our meditation doesn't get lost. Rather, it's just like a doctor's appointment or a work responsibility or anything else: we're booked at that time! We don't have to explain it to anyone, we're just not available then.

Everyone has a sphere of influence, has all kinds of people we interact with everyday and all kinds of choices we make. If we bring even a little more clarity, patience, kindness, honesty, courage, inspiration, or strength—or whatever it is we get from our practice—to those, that's actually a pretty big deal when we really think about it. Particularly in difficult times in the world, how we live our values and engage with those directly around us in our local situations can become all the more precious.

Really, it's up to you. If meditation is helpful in your life, then truly, you're worth it, and the benefit it will have on others around you is worth it too. If you've noticed a difference in yourself—even minutely—then surely that makes a difference for others...especially when we consider the alternatives.

Three Breaths at a Time: On the Spot Practices for Life

Now that we've established a daily meditation practice (or even if we haven't), we've built a reservoir on which we can draw at any moment when we feel like we need it.

One practice I like a lot during the day when I start to get stressed out or upset about something is the practice of three breaths. We can just close our eyes, and take three meditative breaths, then go from there. On the spot meditation.

Or, if there's stronger emotional energy, we can use the same method I wrote about earlier (in "Our Self-Healing, Self-Rejuvenating Mind") where instead of going with our narratives we find the raw feeling in our bodies with curiosity and care, and just breathe with it as if we're massaging a knot in a muscle, in this case, with our breath.

Another practice we can use is to connect with the elements. We can step outside the office for a second, or even look out a window, and gaze into the sky. We can listen to the sounds of nature, and feel the earth beneath us. We can even lay down on the ground for a few minutes and rest this way. We can let the wind and our breath carry away whatever is on our minds, and the warmth of the sun care for what we feel.

We can also practice a walking meditation, where instead of using our breathing as our primary support for meditation, we use our footsteps. We can just pace back and forth like this, and it can be a low-key, calming, centering way to meditate in between activities at work. Before I was a monk, I taught music and performed professionally, and I use to do this in between teaching lessons in schools or on set breaks from gigs.

If we have a long lunch break (and honestly it doesn't seem like many do these days), or a commute that can happen on foot, a nice and easy walk outside can also help.

It also doesn't have to be only at difficult moments when we pause to practice. It can be absolutely anytime we want to come home to ourselves, our peace, our presence, our love, and go from there.

In any case, it's amazing the impact just three breaths can have sometimes. Especially before hitting "send." Or for that matter, before opening the inbox. Or when we get home and turn the car off, to help us really arrive home.

These little "gaps" in life can go such a long way.

Section Two: Journeying into Shamatha

Mindfulness and Awareness

Now that we've covered some basic ground, this next section of chapters will go a little deeper into some of the technical terminology developed in the meditative tradition to help us gain a more precise understanding of our practice. If at any point this gets to be too much, just stop reading, and trust your own experience of your meditation.

There are two natural qualities of mind that are working when we meditate. One is called "mindfulness," and the other is called "awareness."

Mindfulness is what stays with our breath, and *awareness* is what notices when we've become distracted, and also, awareness just understands what's going on in our mind as we practice.

Both are actually just our mind, they're not really two different things, but different terms are used to highlight these different functions.

Sometimes *mindfulness* is also translated as "recollection," or even "remembering." It means to connect with something in a felt way, and to remain, to rest. Emotionally, it's helpful to approach this with a quality of care, ease, and allowance.

Everything is included in our mindfulness. Traditionally, there are "four foundations of mindfulness," which we'll explore in the third section of this book, but the pith is, our bodies, feelings, minds, and the whole world around us are all included within and are foundations for our mindfulness.

This means everything, everything, everything, is welcomed, included, allowed, accepted, exactly the way it is.

Mindfulness is not about getting away from anything, it's about embracing what's there. This is how we reclaim the wholeness of our mind.

Friendliness, acceptance, allowance, emergence, listening, honoring, I think are all very helpful words to point to the spirit or attitude we bring to our mindfulness. Otherwise, our practice can become distant or mechanical, as if there's something to "fix" about ourselves, rather than just coming home to what's already there.

Mindfulness is not something we "do," it's something we *are.* In meditation, we're allowing our mind to rest, to be as it is. We don't need to "focus on our breath," but rather, it's more like *becoming our breath.* The more direct, felt, somatic, intuitive—the better, as this will facilitate a more holistic and grounded approach to our practice, rather than some kind of concentration exercise. This is about trusting ourselves and coming home.

That said, there is a progression involved, and at first, mindfulness—like staying with our breath—does take effort, as we surely know from meditating! But the more we practice, and the more we become familiar with and trust our minds, the more effortless and genuine our mindfulness is revealed to be.

I've written another chapter about effort called "Not Too Tight, Not Too Loose," and will say more about that as we proceed.

Awareness is also a natural function of mind. When we're meditating, it's what notices when we've become distracted, and, it also has introspective understanding of what our mind is doing, like how many and what kinds of thoughts are happening. Sometimes, it's translated as *alertness* or *vigilance*—though again, I'll emphasize that this is something natural and not something we should try too hard to crank up or create.

Often, when we start meditating, we get discouraged by how many thoughts we have, or by how many times we get distracted and have to come back. But, this actually means that *our meditation is working*, and our awareness is working, and *we're doing it right*, because that's what awareness does—it notices what's happening.

In fact, I would say the more times we notice we've been distracted, the better. Every time we notice, we're strengthening our awareness, as if we're lifting weights; every time we notice distraction and come back, we just did a rep. And at first, this is going to happen thousands and thousands of times, even every few breaths. I'll explain more about the progression of stages of meditation in further chapters.

So, when we notice we've been distracted, we can notice with a quality of appreciation, our practice is working, and we're actually already "back to the present" so to speak, so we can just very gently ease back into our breathing. We're reinforcing an extremely valuable lesson: we don't have to be trapped in our thoughts. The more times we do this, the better, and each time, we're learning to trust our awareness a little more. This is a very good thing.

The profound part is that what notices distraction was never itself distracted. What notices we've become caught up in thought was never itself trapped in thought.

There are different levels of awareness. A more dualistic version is what notices thoughts, as if there's a thought, and something noticing, or what notices we've been distracted, as if there was a distraction, and now we're back.

But this is just a tangled version of a more natural, non-dualistic, intuitive, profound awareness. It's an awareness that is our buddha nature shining through, like sun coming through the clouds—the sun was always there.

This kind of awareness is more related to what we call "vipashyana," or, "insight," which is the counterpart to "shamatha," or "calm abiding." We'll explore that more in the chapter called "Shamatha and Vipashyana." The pith of which is: *shamatha* is resting, and *vipashyana* is seeing or having insight. *Shamatha* helps us develop groundedness, clarity, and strength, and then *vipashyana* has insight into the freedom and nature of mind itself.

The reason I mention this now is that awareness is the thread or the bridge between our shamatha, or resting, and our vipashyana, or insight.

A very profound and natural way to ease into vipashyana is, when we notice we've been distracted, we can just relax into, and trust, what noticed.

Connect with that awareness, trust it, and be free. Let the clouds of our thoughts dissolve into the sky of our awareness.

Then if we get spaced out, we still need our breath, so we should come back to that:)

Mindfulness and Permission to Feel

As human beings, we're always feeling. It's what it means to be alive. It connects us with ourselves, each other, and our environment. Feelings, perceptions, and intuitions all contain wisdom.

Yet, these days, we often have to reclaim our ability to truly, actually feel. To *allow* ourselves to feel. To let our systems catch up from bombardment, overwhelm, or oppressive conditionings.

In meditation, we call allowing ourselves to fully connect to our present experience *mindfulness*. Mindfulness is a technical term in meditation that means "to become familiar" with something, to remember it, and to eventually remain undistracted from it. Our bodies, feelings, minds, and the whole world around us are all included within and are foundations for our mindfulness. They're all regarded as sacred.

Everything is welcomed, allowed, and connected with exactly as it is. We're enough, and we can meet life as it is and go from there.

Yet this is something we may have to reclaim through meditation practice, as this natural capacity has often been crushed, overwhelmed, or manipulated through the pace of life and social conditionings. Or, sometimes, our meditation is the first time we've ever realized we *can* feel and connect, especially if we haven't had much of that in our lives. That's OK too, and meditation can be healing in this regard as well.

Technological progress is certainly a good thing, but the frenetic speed of life and business we've harnessed it to create is simply faster than what any normal person can relate with spiritually. We're bombarded with exponentially more information and emotional content every day than we could possibly meaningfully connect with and process. This not only creates a backlog deep within our minds and bodies, but it also leaves our system drained and overtaxed, and the result can be to feel numb, unable to connect or concentrate, slightly anxious, or mildly exhausted.

This is one area where practicing mindfulness in meditation can help, because we're giving our system a chance to rejuvenate, and we're re-empowering that capacity to feel and connect with life that has often been lost in the storm.

We can also revitalize our attention span. When our attention is pulled in a million different directions all the time, again, our system can't really keep up. This fragments our mindfulness and makes it harder to connect and pay attention when we want to, like even with ourselves emotionally, or with our loved ones, or even to take in a lengthy piece of art with appreciation, or to show up with our best qualities in our work. Again, we can repair this by re-cultivating mindfulness in meditation, connecting with our breathing, and allowing our minds to return to a more natural state of ease and health.

Many of us—and the conditionings can be drastically different for everyone—are also affected by one or another social conditioning that says it's OK to feel some things, but not others; or it's OK to express some truths, but not others; or that we have to fake pleasant emotions to get by in a situation, hold back certain painful things, control or manipulate to achieve certain outcomes; and so on. While societal evolution may be needed to heal oppressive dynamics at play, meditation also has a role to play here.

In meditation, part of mindfulness means complete emotional honesty with ourselves. Actually feeling what's there—not what we want it to be, or what any given inner or outer conditioning says it should be, or only the pleasant and not the painful parts—but what's truly there. All of our felt experience has something to teach us, something to hear, and as it untangles from habitual patterns, the wisdom within it can be revealed.

Meditation allows our mindfulness to be set free. It allows this beautiful, natural capacity we have as humans to unfold, to be liberated from fixed narratives, and to embrace every moment of life. It allows us to connect with ourselves and each other more fully, from a wiser, kinder, place, and to understand how to live more true to form.

Even with ourselves, it shows us that it's always possible to connect, and that we're always here. We can give that total acceptance and presence to ourselves, whether or not we have that in our relationships. It can even be an entry into a more unconditional kind of love that we can offer ourselves and others, and that flows through all of life.

The practice of retreat is a highly fortunate situation designed to support this, but ultimately, as we practice, we become increasingly grounded, clear, and strong, and have all the more capacity to relate with whatever may come.

People have been traveling into retreat to meditate together for thousands of years, supporting each other, and ourselves, to rediscover this natural capacity for a sacred way of being.

Grounded, Clear, Strong People: Qualities of Shamatha

As I've mentioned when describing shamatha meditation, there are three natural qualities of mind that are developing more fully as we practice. These are stability, clarity, and strength.

While these refer to our meditation, because we're talking about our own minds and hearts, they refer to ourselves as people. As we practice shamatha, we're becoming increasingly stable or grounded, clear, and strong people. This can change our lives and change our world.

Stability, or groundedness, in meditation means learning to include our whole experience in our breathing, to ground within this present experience, and to become stable. We stay with our breath, or whatever object of meditation we're using. (A mantra, visualization, etc, though in my retreats, I teach the breath as a foundation). We're repairing our attention span, but not just cognitively, also emotionally.

In life, this manifests as being more stable or grounded, present, attentive people. We're less swayed by all the little things that come our way, less prone to wild reactivity, more grounded and present, more patient, more calm, more relaxed, more able to listen to others, more kind, more understanding, and so on. We may feel that we have more space in life, or are a little less trapped in our habitual patterns or reactions, or the volume on our anxiety or stress is a little lower. That is certainly life changing!

The next quality is clarity. In meditation, this means our awareness is getting stronger and we can very clearly see exactly what is happening with the dynamics of our mind and the world around us. But more fundamentally, it's pointing to the actual clarity or capacity for clarity within our minds. We may also experience this as vividness or as the intensity of wakefulness in our meditation, or as beginning to see thoughts before they fully arise.

In life, this means being more clear-minded people. We can see and understand our own patterns, our relationships, other people, and the dynamics of the world around us more clearly or accurately. We can make better decisions, more wise decisions, and we can understand more than we used to be able to understand. We may experience this as an increase in our cognitive or intellectual or creative capacities as well, or as being more skillful in our work. Sometimes, after we've meditated for a while, we have fresh insight into our lives and our worldview.

Stability and clarity can also mean we're less easily fooled by the constant attempts to manipulate us or keep our world view myopic and self-affirming that whichever particular media outlet or social media feed we subscribe to is typically reinforcing. We may be able to see the world in more subtly and dynamic interdependent relationship than "my side is right, the other side is wrong, and all the problems are their fault." We may begin to self-reflect more and see our complicity in many of the issues we care about, and we may see more clearly how to take helpful action. And, we may begin to understand how societal and systemic dynamics are happening, and how different people come to different views, which are helpful and which are harmful, and how to help more at the root levels in sincere ways.

This kind of meditative stability and clarity is something our world desperately needs. Far too often, we're so trapped in cycles of blame and reactivity that we can't see beneath the surface and into deeper roots of issues, nor how to help in meaningful ways. It's not unusual at all for those of us who develop a serious meditation practice to end up making major changes in our lives as a result of coming to greater clarity about how we can live in meaningful alignment with our wisdom, intuition, compassion, and purpose. Or, we continue to do exactly what we already do, but we can do so with greater capacity and understanding.

The next quality is strength. In meditation, this refers to becoming more immovable, potent, strong, and even powerful in our practice. We're able to harness the full energy of our minds, and direct it how we choose. It's a result of deeper meditation, in which our mind literally becomes stronger.

In life, this manifests as being stronger or more resilient people, and as having greater capacity and power in whatever we do. This is something we will all need as conditions in our world continue to get more challenging.

If, as we practice meditation a little bit each day over months or years, any of these qualities are developing even microscopically, then our practice is working. If we feel even ever so slightly more calm or grounded, ever so slightly less easily swayed, just even a little more patient, a little more clear; if we understand a bit more than we did before, and if we have new insight into how our lives are working, and more resiliency, or if we can handle more than we used to, then it's working:)

We often underestimate how profound and life-changing even microscopic progress in our own meditation practice can be for others within our spheres of influence. It's actually a big deal.

One of the first times I attended a meditation gathering, what struck me was that the teacher I encountered was actually listening to me. She was actually seeing me, and connecting with me, and listening to what I was saying. She had that kind of space in her mind, she wasn't just waiting to talk. That's why I stayed at that Dharma center back in Texas where I'm from; I kept coming back, and well, got a little carried away I guess:)

In the retreats I lead now, I've been so inspired by working with people from a wide range of life situations. I've heard physicians and healthcare practitioners say their meditation practice helps them to make more accurate diagnoses, or to treat their patients with more kindness. I've heard C-Suite executives and high-powered business folks say they're more patient with the large numbers of people who work for them and they make more skillful decisions. On multiple occasions, I have seen some people change their job to utilize their influence in more positive ways. I've seen educators find fresh inspiration and ways to uplift their students. I've worked with lots of people who became or remained sober with help from meditation. I've worked with countless people who serve in a wide array of helping professions, and credit meditation with part of their own self-care and how they recharge, keep going, and don't burn out. And more.

When we think about it, that's quite a contribution to a brighter world that our meditation practice can have. Even if we may think we're doing it for ourselves, our meditation practice can make a difference. The world certainly needs as many grounded, clear, strong people as it can get, especially as we continue to navigate major changes, and difficult outcomes from our previous collective actions.

But personally, my favorite anecdote about the benefits of meditation came from a great Tibetan master who ran a large monastery in Asia, where thousands of people would ordain as monastics during their younger years, while the majority would train for a while and then disrobe and return to household life in their twenties or thirties. Another teacher asked him why he continued to ordain and train so many, knowing most would leave.

He said, "Because they'll make better parents."

Not Too Tight, Not Too Loose

In ancient India, there was a stringed instrument similar to what became the sitar, guitar, that sort of thing. A musician who played one went to the Buddha and asked, "How do I hold my mind when I meditate?". The Buddha responded, "How do you tune your strings on your instrument?". The musician said, "Well, if they're too tight, they'll pop off and break, and if they're too loose, they won't make a sound, so they have to be not too tight and not too loose." The Buddha said "Yes, like that." I'm paraphrasing anyway, we have 2600 years of telephone game at this point...

This essentially means that we need to try just hard enough to meditate, but not too hard.

In meditation, we're always working with a very natural process, because innately, we're awake.

At first, we just need to tune into our breathing enough to allow our mind to settle down, so that this can eventually be revealed.

Were I to emotionally translate "not too tight, not too loose," I would say, "engaged, yet relaxed." I would say we're balancing engagement or effort with relaxation and ease. Eventually, they return to being one, and to being natural. We're training to come home to what's always been there.

If we try too hard to meditate, we'll have a few glorious moments of clarity, then, before we know it, we're wildly distracted with some fantasy, or we're furiously angry, or claustrophobic. The strings pop off.

In meditative terminology, this is the result of being too tight, and is called wildness, restlessness, craziness, or "elation," though I'm not sure that's the right choice of English words as it can mean more "overjoyed," which isn't at all the meaning here. The sense is that our meditation is not sustainable because we're trying too hard, so our mind rebels. We can't rest.

Or, worse, every time that happens, we might feel like we're not trying hard enough to meditate because "we can't do it right, we're thinking too much," and then we try even harder and our practice becomes a frustrating cycle of perceived failure and self-criticism.

We don't have to do that to ourselves! As we've discussed, our meditation is a natural process, it's coming home to what we are.

So, if we find ourselves getting frustrated or self-critical in our practice, it may mean that we're trying too hard and we can afford to relax and give ourselves more space.

We can ease up by raising our gaze a little, focusing more on our outbreath and relaxing into it, loosening our hold on our breath so to speak, or also warming up a little physically by going out to sit in the sun.

On the other hand, if we start to get spaced out, drowsy (but not physically tired), especially after we've been meditating for a while, or in retreats; if we feel mildly daydreamy, kind of pleasantly sedated, this can mean we've relaxed too much and are "too loose," and the result is called "laxity."

This "laxity" can actually be deceptive, because it feels really good. It's a little like reclining back on our couch with YouTube on in the background with the volume kind of low, and maybe some kind of recreational beverage is involved.

Our mind has basically settled down, we're not struggling to meditate or stay with the breath, so that's a good thing, but we've relaxed a little bit too much and we've started to sink into a sedated state of mind.

In terms of the three qualities of shamatha; groundedness or stability, clarity, and strength, we might be settled, but we're not clear.

When we feel this way, we need more engagement. We can perk up by straightening our posture a bit, tuning into the breathing more closely, maybe bringing the gaze a bit lower, and sharpening our awareness. We just need to perk up our meditation, and lean in a little more.

The sign that we're adjusted properly would be that we regain a bit more clarity in our meditation, but that we can still relax, we haven't gone too far the other direction and become frustrated.

In many of my longer retreats, we do an experiential exercise in which we intentionally gradually get too tight and then too loose, and gradually adjust, so that we can gain our own intuitive understanding of how each feels and how to adjust, and how to relax into natural ease and engagement.

That may be a little tricky to try without guidance, but I hope the above gives a basic idea, and you can definitely use the tips included in this chapter to make adjustments and see what happens.

As always, the path of meditation is about getting to know our minds.

All of us have our own habitual patterns, karmic tendencies, personalities, and conditionings. Some of us will habitually be a little tight, and some will habitually be a little loose. And, at the same time, when I talk later about "Stages of Shamatha Meditation," I'll describe how working with tightening and loosening, or engagement and relaxation, is also its own process, and it goes different ways as our meditation deepens and we continue to adjust.

If we have a job or a lifestyle that demands extreme precision under stress, high work volume, very little margin for error with high consequences, then very often (and for good reason), we may habitually run a little tight in our meditation and likely need to give ourselves permission to relax a little. Or, if we have perfectionistic tendencies, same thing.

This can definitely be a journey for folks who are used to being able to do everything right the first time, or for whom "failure" is not an option. It's very sad, because it can often lead to a lot of unnecessary struggle, pain, and self-criticism in meditation and that will actually be counterproductive!

So if it helps at all, we can think "relaxing more and giving myself more space is actually doing it right. That's how this works. The proper way to meditate is to be friendly to myself, trust my mind, and let it work over time."

That said, it can also go the other way, where if we have to be in high gear all the time at work, then we come into our meditation kind of emotionally exhausted and we just flop, and end up being too loose. If this happens, we probably need to give ourselves more rest and transition time. Like maybe take a nap or a walk before we meditate, or if we go on retreat, let ourselves just rest and take it easy the first day or so, and then practice once we feel a bit more rejuvenated. (And yeah, we might need more than a day or two...but that's another discussion).

If we tend to run too tight habitually, it can also be helpful to meditate after we exercise, or late at night when we're a little worn out.

On the other hand, if we have too much space and down time in our lives, like we've been laid off work, or we just retired and haven't found our flow yet, or we're putting off school for the umpteenth time, or we've become a little depressed or fallen into a rut, then we may run a little loose in our meditation.

As in life, or in a relationship, there are times we need more space (loosening up), and there are times we need to bring things back to life, engage, lean in, find the spark, the love, the magic, again (engaging more or tightening up a little). Said another way, there are times we need to chill, and times we need to work:)

So, if we're running a little loose in our meditation, then we may need to bring more heartfelt discipline or engagement to our practice. It can be helpful to remember our intention or motivation at the beginning of our practice, like why we decided to meditate in the first place, and really connect with that in a heartfelt way, set up a special place to practice with images and things that inspire us, and set realistic goals like relatively short sessions of meditation where we really feel like we have the energy for it.

As much as part of me kind of hates to say it, a cup of tea or coffee might not be a bad idea either, as long as we know that's a crutch to give us a little more juice with which to engage in our practice—caffeine alone has nothing to do with how we adjust our meditation in terms of tightening or loosening. And on the other hand, if we tend to run too tight or perfectionistic as I mentioned earlier, it can be helpful to cut back a little or meditate when we're decaffeinated, while again, that itself is not the answer.

We'll talk a lot more about these themes, but for now, this is a good start.

Stages of Shamatha Meditation

Meditation is a natural process, and like any process, it goes through stages.

This is an extremely rich topic in meditation, and there are thick volumes passed down for millennia that go into incredible detail about it. For now, my goal in this chapter is just to give some broad strokes, pithy guidance, and some natural and easy-to-intuit images to describe the process.

When we first sit down to meditate, the image used to describe our mind is a waterfall!

This is exactly what it sounds like. We sit down, and we're totally overwhelmed or overcome by tons and tons of thoughts. And usually, these will be very surface-level thoughts, like things we've been thinking about through the day, things we just did, need to do, worries and dramas and such, that are on our mind. Like a waterfall, it just carries us right away. We may be with our breath for a few seconds, but them bam, we're back to thinking about work, family, whatever.

Congratulations, our meditation is working!

No, really, it's working. Our mindfulness has been placed on our breath, and our awareness has noticed that we have a tremendous amount of thoughts that are carrying us away all the time. This is literally par for the course, it's on the map. At this point, we may feel like we have even more thoughts than usual, but really, we're just noticing what's been happening most of the time in our minds throughout the day.

The thing to do is continue to just gently mix our mind with our breathing, and continue to welcome all of our thoughts and emotional content into our breath, into the feeling of our body breathing, just very gently bringing ourselves into the arena of meditation and including the contents of our mind in our practice. We can let ourselves really feel the texture of our breath, our body breathing, and any emotional energy within the thoughts.

The trick is to neither "indulge" nor "follow" all of the thoughts by believing them and getting caught up in the stories, nor "repress" by trying to make them go away or not feel the underlying emotional energy. Rather, just *include*, and *feel*, and *welcome* it all into the breath directly, and mix our mind with our breathing, *become our breathing*, and allow the movement of the water to mix with its clarity and begin to settle.

The term in meditation is "placement," as in "placing our mind on the breath," and what it means is to deliberately engage with our breathing, and give our mind to our breathing, give our allegiance to our breathing, mix our whole being with and become our breathing. As we do this, the habitual patterns of thought will gradually lose their power because we're not giving them our energy by following or indulging them into all the stories, nor repressing as if there were something real to get away from.

"Placement" is the first of what are described as the nine stages of shamatha meditation. Then, the next stages are called "continual placement" and "repeated placement".

This is also pretty much what it sounds like. As we mix our mind with our breathing, very gradually we're able to do so for a little longer, like maybe we stay with our breathing for a few more breaths before becoming distracted. It happens little by little, as very gradually, we're with our breath for a bit longer, we can gradually rest with our breathing a bit more. Our "placement" lasts a little longer, and becomes "continual placement."

Then, what happens? We keep getting distracted, and we keep coming back!

That's actually a very good thing. Every time we notice we're distracted, that's our *awareness* working and doing its job, and then our mindfulness can return to and remain with our breath.

We do this over, and over, and over again. Breathing, noticing we've become distracted, and gently coming back to our breath.

The more times that happens the better, because we're strengthening our trust in awareness and learning that we don't have to be trapped in our thoughts and habitual patterns like a prison of our own mind. We have the power to notice, to make a choice, and to simply be present and allow the thoughts to dissolve into the space from which they came. Every time we notice we're distracted and come back, it's like a step in a march towards our freedom, or a rep in an exercise. So have at it!

This process of noticing and coming back over and over again is "repeated placement," or in some translations, "continuously resettling the mind."

As we do so, gradually, our mind may be less like a waterfall and more like a running river. There's still a strong current, lots of movement, and we're still getting pulled away a lot, but we're basically able to navigate the waters and correct course with our raft, so to speak.

The contents of our thoughts may also start to go a little beneath the surface, like not necessarily what we were just thinking about or doing throughout the day, but they may start to wander with a little more space, and they may not be quite so loud.

Or, conversely, this is also where a lot of strong emotional energy may begin to surface, though as I'll describe in another chapter called "Cycles of Stabilizing and Instigating," that can happen at any point as our practice deepens and we access or interrupt deeper levels of emotional energy beneath what we usually can in daily life. In terms of how to work with strong emotional energy when it does arise, there's an earlier chapter called "Our Self-Healing, Self-Rejuvenating Mind," which gives some tips.

This stage of "repeated placement," or noticing distraction and coming back over and over again, is also where "too tight" can very quickly become an issue, as we can get frustrated with having to bring our minds back over and over again, and can get into a vicious cycle of trying too hard, our mind rebelling, popping off into fantasy or self-aggression, irritation, anger, etc., and then trying even harder...please don't do that to yourself:)

Rather, like calming down an upset child or pet, this is where we may actually need to give our mind a little more space, let the thoughts be there, include their energy in the wider space of our breathing, feel them, and like holding an upset child or pet, gradually allow them to settle. And if they do need to just run around a bit, well OK, we're watching, and we'll notice, and we'll keep coming back.

As we've discussed in working with "too tight," we can also focus more on our outbreath, dissolve out with it more, relax into it more, relax into the space in the room and our sense perceptions a bit more, raise our gaze a little, or warm up physically a bit one way or another.

This may go on for quite a while. In our daily meditation practice, this may more or less be what we're working with, and that's all well and good! As we've discussed, we're strengthening our mindfulness and awareness through this process, and that will have real and tangible benefits in our lives. These first few stages of meditation can make an enormous difference in our quality of life. As our practice matures, or especially in retreat settings, we may begin to work with some of what I'll describe next.

At some point, our mind basically stabilizes or becomes grounded, and it's more like a lake than a river. A lake still has all kinds of ripples and things on the surface, might have rivers flowing into and out of it, but it's basically a lake. Our mind is relatively stable or grounded in our breathing and our present experience.

This is also where "too loose" can be an issue: we settle down a little too much, and it's like we start sinking into the lake and drifting around in all the little currents. We're basically calmed down, and "too loose" tends to feel good, so we may feel quite content to daydream a little or space out a bit while more or less being with our breathing. Like the laxity I described earlier.

At this point, we need to engage a bit more, or toughen up our awareness a little, bring all of that mental content into the sphere or our awareness, and strengthen our mindfulness. We can hold our breath a bit closer, like really tuning into it more, straighten up our posture, open a window, or dress a bit lighter (let in the cold).

As we're able to remain steadily with our breathing, navigate low-level thought activity, but no longer become completely distracted to the point we're not with the breath at all but totally in our thoughts or stories, we've begun to develop the fourth stage of shamatha, "close placement," or "fully settling the mind."

At this point, in terms of the qualities of shamatha, of groundedness or stability, clarity, and strength, we've basically developed stability so much so that often the breath kind of falls away and the mind is resting firmly within itself. Now we begin to work more with clarity.

This is also the point where we may work with what many meditators describe as the "undercurrent," meaning a more subtle level of thought beneath the surface, like a calm or even frozen lake on top with some movement and fish and things swimming around beneath. The trick is to include them in our awareness and continue to toughen up the edges a bit, engage a bit more, rather than getting pulled into this undercurrent of thought (indulging), nor trying to pretend it isn't there (repressing).

All of our thoughts are our mind, and there's a lot of creative energy and wisdom within them. As we bring this more subtle level of thought into our awareness and contact it directly, the conceptual aspect can liberate while the energy can be harnessed into our meditation, into our mindfulness. Otherwise, it's like we're leaking a little energy out the bottom, and if enough seeps in, we start to sink. This is a relatively subtle process, but we're regaining the wholeness of our minds, and really engaging in our practice with our whole heart.

As we learn we can engage completely, give our whole heart to our practice, bring our full mindfulness and awareness to bear, our mind perks up and develops more clarity and joy. The fifth stage of shamatha is called "taming the mind," and we're working with and overcoming this more subtle level of "too loose," or "laxity," which otherwise leaves some raw energy on the table that we'll need to gather and include to go farther.

At this point, our mind is like a crystal-clear lake; we can see in all directions, and the water is vivid, joyful, refreshing, and life giving. In terms of the three qualities of shamatha (stability, clarity, strength), we've been stable for some time now, ie, not really going anywhere, and are becoming more clear. All of our energy is being harnessed into our practice.

As things progress from here, we practice with increasingly subtle layers of mind, not nearly as loud or coarse as before, and accordingly, a more refined tightening or loosening, or engagement and relaxation. What we're doing is drawing all of the energy of our mind together, and relaxing within that. This takes exertion and perseverance, as it can be easy to just settle and then gradually backslide. Through that harnessing of our full potential, we begin to feel the strength and power of our mind coming to bear.

As it does, well beyond thought, our mind rests within itself with gravity, depth, power. The obstacles though this process can be either "not applying the antidotes" where we just rest under laurels so to speak, or "overapplying the antidotes" where we keep meddling around unnecessarily instead of trusting our mind enough to relax.

As strength and power develop, we can trust that, like feeling the engines on a plane taking us up into the air. We can relax and let go. Meditation is effortless. We're just resting naturally.

These latter stages I just described are called "pacifying the mind," "completely pacifying the mind," "one-pointedness," and finally, "equanimity"—-where meditation becomes completely effortless.

Our minds are like a vast ocean, and eventually, totally immovable and powerful, like a mountain.

As this comes together with vipashyana, our mind is like the sky, which it's always been.

Those more advanced stages are beyond what most of us will work with in shorter or even longer retreats.

My goal here was to paint some broad strokes and provide some pithy guidance for practice. That said, there's a LOT more material and detail on the stages of shamatha that I didn't go into now which are found in traditional texts and from guidance by realized meditation masters.

So, if you'd like to learn more at any point, I'd recommend a book called *The Path of Tranquility and Insight* by Khenchen Thrangu Rinpoche.

In that book, he is teaching from a volume of Jamgon Kongtrul's *Treasury of Knowledge*, which is a classic and vast encyclopedia of

Buddhist wisdom that we study from frequently in traditional educations.

If you connect with Chögyam Trungpa Rinpoche, you may also enjoy the section, "Part Three: Meditation and Samadhi" within his book *The Path of Individual Liberation*, which is one of three volumes of many classic Buddhist teachings he gave.

Cycles of Stabilizing and Instigating: Calm, and Emotional Eruptions

Our meditation practice will go through cycles of stabilizing and instigating, or said another way, times when we're basically calming down and becoming more stable, and times when there are eruptions of emotional energy. These may be things from our past or even childhood (and from a Buddhist point of view, multiple past lifetimes as well...).

Or, they may be entirely new ways of looking at life, all kinds of fresh energy, new perspectives, inspirations, ideas, and so on. These can also come along with a wide array of physical sensations, and with or without any emotional material at all.

These can be disorienting or confusing experiences especially if we don't know to expect them, which is why I'm writing this chapter, and also talk about this in retreats.

The way this works is that all of our unprocessed emotional material is stored deep within our minds and bodies. This is far beneath the surface level of mind that we use on a daily basis, and while these old patterns, experiences, traumas, and emotional material are *very much* influencing the way we experience life now, we may or may not encounter the raw material directly in daily life. It's stored at a much more subtle level.

In Western psychology and science, we may look at this as the unconscious or deeper elements of our psyche, or as the way our brain and nervous system work, how they've been conditioned, and so on. I'll stay in my lane here because, in Buddhism, we look at it as different levels of consciousness, which also have an energetic component in our bodies.

From a Buddhist point of view, everything we've ever experienced is stored within deep levels of our consciousness, which in turn, is stored within and influences the patterning of the energetic body that determines our experience of life.

As we practice meditation, our mind is settling, and our awareness is gradually deepening. Typically, we experience this as our minds calming down a bit, and developing the stability or groundedness, clarity, and strength that we've talked a good bit about in *shamatha* meditation.

This is usually what we'd expect from meditation. We practice, and gradually, we feel better.

That said, there's another thing happening at the same time, as we meditate, and our awareness deepens. It can also encounter all of this emotional material, which is stored farther down in our minds and bodies than what we normally relate with on a day-to-day basis.

We may experience this in meditation retreats, where we practice for a while, and then suddenly we're sobbing about an old break up, or furious about a childhood injury, or a situation from a long time ago. Or, we may just be overcome with emotion and have no idea what it's about.

This is a totally natural part of meditation practice, and nothing is wrong.

On the contrary, as I wrote in "Our Self-Healing, Self-Rejuvenating Mind," this is actually our opportunity to do what we weren't able to do back then: feel the raw emotional energy fully, with presence, gentleness, and groundedness within our breath and the sensory world around us, and allow it to open up, heal, and release.

The way I recommend working with this is to not pay much attention to the conceptual narratives, and not try to "figure them out," rationalize, or further ruminate on them. There may be value in that, but it will likely not get to the root of the blockage. Rather, *get curious about where the raw emotional energy is in the body, and how it feels.*

While every experience will be unique, a few examples of this may be like anger that is tight in the chest, or like lead in the stomach, or an emotional wound that's like a pain in the heart, and so on.

In terms of meditative physiology, when we aren't able to process emotional material completely at the time we experienced it, or if it's a type of experience we've replayed many times and formed patterns around, it forms a blockage in the flow of the energetic body.

The way to heal this is to bring our minds to it now with complete acceptance, love, trust, and curiosity. Where is it in our body? How does it feel? What is it made of? Can I breathe space into it?

I think of this as like massaging a knot in a muscle, but with our breathing. Really breathing with the raw energy, and breathing space into it, and even mixing it with the space around us in the room as we breathe out.

A sign that we're going in a healthy direction is that the energy is fundamentally opening up. There may still be conceptual stories, thoughts, mental images, and so on, but they have a bit less hold on us, the volume is a bit lower, a little less overwhelming. The stories may even change and start to reflect a greater understanding, or they may dissolve altogether. Physically, we can feel the stuckness loosening, melting, opening, dissolving.

This may feel easy, or it may feel intense and cathartic, and it may involve tears. Crying can be very healthy, and that's why there are boxes of tissues in meditation halls.

If it feels overwhelming, we may need to ground ourselves more in the physical world around us, like taking in the sights and sounds in the room, and connecting with whichever of our senses feels grounded and safe, and holding the experience within that greater space. Again, gradually breathing with the raw energy, mixing it with that greater space, and allowing it to release and dissolve.

The sign that we're not going in a healthy direction would be that we feel trapped within the old thoughts, patterns, memories, experiences, as if we were reliving them, and struggling with them, or even just getting pulled right back in and reinforcing them in a stronger way.

If this happens, despite anything we try, meditation may not be the right tool at this moment. We may need to just get up and go out for a walk, talk with a friend or instructor, or do whatever we find helpful in working with intense emotional energy. If we're in any kind of a therapeutic process, it can be helpful to speak with our therapist before entering retreat and be sure it feels like a good fit right now; or, to have a strategy for when meditation can surface intense material, particularly trauma. If this is becoming difficult, it can be helpful to stick to shorter sessions of meditation, and there are all kinds of ways the meditation technique itself can be altered or adjusted to be more supportive. This can be helpful to speak with an instructor about. Please don't just try to sit through it!

That said, these releases of energy that occur as meditation deepens can also be quite pleasant, and can sometimes involve feelings of joy, physical bliss, energetic openings in the body, and can come along with all sorts of different experiences. In those cases, the trick is to just let them occur, let them pass on through, and not get too fascinated. Again, it's a normal part of meditation, and nothing is wrong.

What's happening is that our mindfulness and awareness are becoming stronger, flowing through our bodies, and encountering places where the energy is stuck, helping it release, and returning to a more natural flow. As this happens, there can be all kinds of little side effects.

We may also have a totally different kind of experience, where as we meditate, we have surges of new energy, new ideas, big inspirations, new ways of looking at the world. This can also be a sign that our practice is encountering and opening up old blocked energy, and a surge of new energy is being released.

While these may ultimately lead to positive changes in our lives, it's important not to get too carried away at first. Often, advice is given to not make major life decisions in retreats, because when the energy first opens up, it can be like a dam bursting, and may not be a settled, healthy flow. So, instead, as we continue to practice, we can trust that whatever wisdom is there will only become more clear over time, so we don't need to hurry or make any rash decisions. We will come to our own clarity, and we will know what to do.

It may also be helpful in meditation retreats, and in our life generally, to incorporate some kind of a healthy emotional or creative outlet. Some people write poetry, create art, journal, and so on, to help facilitate a positive way to process what comes up in our meditation and life.

These cycles of stabilizing and instigating can not only play out in a given session or period of meditation, but also in phases of our meditative life cycle. We may have many years at a time when our practice is only stabilizing, and nothing like I've been describing is occurring at all. That's totally fine! And, we may then have whole phases of life where these things are occurring more intensely.

In these more instigating cycles, it can be important to have guidance and support from friends, mentors, and meditation instructors, in order to process the experiences socially and ensure they're being channeled in healthy directions.

And, as you might expect, they are indeed cycles, as the more stable and deep our practice becomes, the more profound levels we work with.

But for sure, on the whole, our practice should always be lessening our confusion, and leading to more wisdom, compassion, and openness. It may be a messy process at times, but that should always be the general direction, especially over the long term.

Rousing Motivation, and Believing in Ourselves

Often, traditional texts about meditation describe a series of obstacles and antidotes that we encounter and progress through as we practice. I've woven some of these into previous chapters. But, the first obstacle is one I'm sure we all know quite well: getting to the cushion to begin with.

Life these days is definitely very busy. The general pace has absolutely sped up and become more intense for the vast majority of the population than it was in ancient times, aside from people being exploited in choiceless and endless work, or locked in cycles of violence and survival.

So, understandably, many of us struggle to get to the cushion.

What I recommend as a starting point is to have an honest reflection and conversation with ourselves.

First, why do we meditate? Why have we chosen to do this? Since we've been doing it (if for at least one year), what difference has it made in our lives?

If we've found meditation beneficial—even a little—and it's something that we've chosen to incorporate into our lives, we can absolutely trust ourselves and our direct experience, and believe in ourselves.

We are in fact doing it, and it's working.

Then, the next step is allocating and protecting a realistic, attainable, and inspiring amount of time to dedicate to our practice.

As I wrote in an earlier chapter "Daily Practice: Our Reservoir of Sanity," I actually recommend low balling it. Pick an amount of time that feels attainable and inspiring on even the busiest day. An amount that we can feel like, "Oh yeah, I could do that no problem, in fact, I could do more!" That's the right amount. Because then, we'll do it consistently and feel good about it, even build momentum and confidence. And then, when we're able, we can certainly always extend our session longer on some days, but when we get too busy, we won't feel bad for not getting to it at all.

Then, we need to pick a time during the day that we can realistically allocate for meditation, but once we pick it, we need to protect it. If we wait to meditate once life has slowed down, we'll die waiting. And when we do, our boss won't go with us, nor will anything we needed to do, but our state of mind will.

I recommend treating our meditation time like any other appointment. Just put it in our phone or calendar, and then "we're booked then." It's as simple as that. That's our time to meditate, in the same way that we may have a time for a particular work meeting, personal appointment, or family responsibility.

Traditionally, meditation texts—and they're not trying to insult us, they're speaking from experience—describe three types of "laziness" that keep us from getting to the cushion. One is having lost heart, another is being too stuck in habitual patterns, and the last is having too many activities. In other words, not feeling like it, getting discouraged, being too stuck in our usual routines, or having too much to do.

We can overcome these not only with the strategy for daily practice I just described, but also by rekindling our motivation.

Sparking our motivation can be helpful not only in getting to the cushion, but also as we begin our meditation practice in each session. This can be especially true when we've been practicing for a while, or in retreat settings, where it can be easy to lose the forest for the trees and just kind of sink into our usual meditative mood, which can become a rut, and can inhibit our practice from continuing to grow and flourish.

Recalling, or rousing, our motivation works to the extent that it's truly meaningful and heartfelt to us. So really, why have we started meditating at all? Why have we chosen to do this? And since we've been doing it, what difference has it made in our lives? What difference do we aspire for it to make for others, and for the world?

Connecting with this in a sincere way can be how we find the love, the spark, the magic, in our practice.

Once we do, we can then very deliberately begin to meditate, as in, "and for that reason, now I'll begin to mix my mind with my breathing and meditate."

If we've reflected and found that our practice has had a meaningful impact on our lives or on those around us, we really can trust that, and let it carry us farther, like raising the sail on a ship.

Section Three: Vipashyana and the Four Foundations of Mindfulness

Shamatha and Vipashyana

To this point, I've mainly been describing *shamatha* or "peaceful abiding meditation," which is how we make peace with ourselves and rest with groundedness, clarity, and strength. Shamatha meditation can be a foundation of a healthy life, and certainly of a prosperous spiritual path. It predated Buddhism by a long shot, and was something the historical Buddha Shakyamuni learned from his own teachers.

Vipashyana, or "insight" meditation, also existed in some forms before the Buddha's time, but it's where he went further into his own breakthrough to the complete freedom we call "enlightenment." This is nothing more and nothing less than coming home forever to one's own innate wisdom, compassion, and openness, or Buddha Nature, and releasing all the temporarily tangled afflictive emotions and patterns of actions (*klesha* and *karma*) that have kept us trapped in prisons of our own making.

One analogy is of clouds dissolving back into the sky and the sun illuminating everything, churning oceans of love. Then we help others, more and more.

While vipashyana expresses more of the Buddha's view, it can also be practiced by anyone at all, whether or not we want to become a Buddhist. In fact, many of the exact techniques I'll be discussing are often adapted or drawn from in secular mindfulness programs, apps, books, and so on, as well as in Buddhist training.

This is because while shamatha is about resting, vipashyana is about seeing, having insight, and setting our minds and hearts free from the limiting patterns in which they've been temporarily trapped. *It's about understanding our own minds* and worlds, and reclaiming our own birthright—freedom. It's not about adding anything.

There are many levels of vipashyana. Some are more "worldly" meaning they're more to do with understanding how our minds and the world works, understanding the dynamics and patterns at play, understanding cause and effect in more and more subtle, complex, and accurate ways, rather than necessarily anything more unconditional or profound.

That said, obviously, that can be life changing and enormously helpful! Many of us experience this naturally as we meditate and spend time becoming familiar with our minds and becoming increasingly grounded, clear, and strong. From that, we gain insight into life. For example, the way that a particular story line in our minds leads us around for better or worse; the particular conditionings we've had in our lives, and where they came from; the dynamics of how a relationship is occurring; or clarity about what to do in a given situation in terms of what is helpful and what isn't.

This is, in some ways, a maturation of those same natural qualities of clarity and awareness we've discussed before.

As this continues to unfold, it becomes a more unconditional kind of vipashyana that's more about the thinking, grasping mind unfurling into its nature of infinitely open, expansive, loving presence. Revealing buddha nature. We call it "unconditional" because it's always there, based on nothing at all, and never ceasing—even through birth and death.

Vipashyana's insight means intuitively, confidently, experiencing that our mind is not truly real, let alone trapped in thought. Rather, it is empty of such confines and confusion, yet full of boundless wisdom and love. Even thoughts, afflictive emotions, habitual patterns, are fleeting, changing, and have only ever been as solid as we've made them. They're free of their own accord.

While this is beyond words, an image is the open sky.

When we rest as buddha nature effortlessly, with stability, clarity, and strength, shamatha and vipashyana have returned to their natural union. This happens a little at a time, and generally, the better our shamatha, and the more we trust ourselves and put our heart in it, the more we're able to rest in vipashyana. I'll say more about that as we proceed.

Vipashyana is what liberates us or sets our minds free, and one way it can work is that when we have insight into how we're stuck, immediately we're no longer stuck. Chögyam Trungpa Rinpoche said, "That which sees confusion is not itself confused."

I've been weaving this in a bit as we've been going along thus far, encouraging us to always trust what notices that we've been distracted and simply relax into that, expand out, and let go. This is one way to practice vipashayana.

Another is by mixing our minds with our outbreaths, and dissolving out into space with each outbreath, again allowing our minds to relax and let go. Very natural, expansive. There is a whole chapter about this called "Mixing Mind, Breath, and Space," a little later in this series which you can jump to if you're curious.

The following section of chapters weaves together what are called the "Four Foundations of Mindfulness" with both shamatha and vipashyana instructions, as is traditional. Especially when we get to mindfulness of mind in a few chapters here, I'll say quite a lot more about practicing vipashyana, and will emphasize it there with some easy to use techniques like the ones I just mentioned and more. That said, that's just my own particular style, and any of the four can absolutely be used as a basis for vipashyana, even eventually, they all will.

Four Foundations of Mindfulness: Everything Is Included

The Four Foundations of Mindfulness are a traditional teaching on how to welcome and include absolutely everything in our practice. They are our bodies, feelings, minds, and the whole world around us. Pretty much sums it up, right? All of those are regarded as quite sacred, waiting to be fully discovered.

There are many different ways of approaching the vast teachings on the Four Foundations of Mindfulness, and my own brief writings here are in no way meant to be complete or definitive. Rather, they're intended as a gentle and direct guide for one way that we can bring these into our practice, based on what I've seen be helpful for folks I work with and in my own little practice.

In the Art of Meditation: Weeklong Retreat, which I lead, and other longer retreats (longer than a weekend), I'll often lead us through these one by one, which is one way we can practice these.

However, it's also totally fine to just allow the spirit of these to naturally infuse our practice, or to turn to the teachings on any of them for guidance in working with all kinds of things they may be helpful for at any point.

There is no need to try to "do" all of this, and if, at any point, reading these it feels like too much, just stop reading and trust your own experience of meditation and your own wisdom on how to proceed.

This next series of chapters will proceed through the four foundations of mindfulness: body, feelings, mind, and phenomenal world, inviting us to include more and more in our practice, and to invite the curiosity of vipashyana into the journey of revealing our nature.

Scanning Our Precious Body

Our human bodies are incredibly precious and sacred. If we look around, even on our one little planet Earth, they're actually very rare. The insects (let alone bacteria!) and animals have us dramatically outnumbered, and while they may have a lot to teach us about living in harmony with the environment, they spend most of their time trying to get enough to eat and not be eaten. And who knows how many other kinds of life exist?

We humans, well, we certainly have our own problems...but if we're fortunate enough to have the kind of life situation that allows us to sit around reading about meditation, or even practicing in retreats or at home, then we likely have abundant blessings to count, and a lot of ability to help others. That said, in the history of meditation it's amazing how practitioners have been able to continue and embody the teachings in truly dire circumstances like prison, war, and exile. That is the power of the human mind.

Our bodies make this, and all of our life, possible. They're made from the elements of the earth, our parents, and are home to our minds. They can give life, sustain life, even help create life. It's so incredibly sacred and powerful, these bodies of ours. They're the temple we have in every moment of life, which we can come home to and rest in.

Our bodies are changing all the time, instant by instant in dynamic relationship with the world around us, and of course, will not last forever and will return home to the earth when we die. They can even become sustenance for other beings if we choose a natural burial, or prolong the lives of other people if we're able and willing to donate organs, or to research which can help people in other ways, or to give ourselves and our loved ones peace by following our and their wishes.

Our bodies are a sacred part of the ecosystem, one with the circle of life.

Our bodies are also amazing supports for our meditation practice. It can be helpful to take time to really ground ourselves in our bodies as we begin to practice, and I'll guide us through a technique for that called a "body scan."

Body scans can be especially helpful if we spend a lot of time "stuck in our heads" at work, on social media, and so on. Or, if we work with a lot of anxiety, grounding ourselves in our body is often helpful. A body scan is also a skillful means to harness the energy of a very busy or active mind as we come into meditation, kind of giving it something to do, so to speak, rather than immediately trying to settle into the breath which can be a bit jarring or claustrophobic at times, like trying to stop rather than ride a wave.

Body scans are an invitation to total acceptance and friendliness with the body we have.

These days, I don't even need to mention how much harmful, manipulative messaging there is coming at us constantly—and of course different depending who we are—telling us our body should or shouldn't be this or that way, and just buy or do this to make it conform more (isn't that convenient?), and so on.

Body scans can be a healing way of reclaiming every single inch of the sacredness of our own bodies, exactly the way we are.

We are worthy and complete from the moment we're born. No one can sell us that, nor take that away. It's literally our birthright. We can reclaim it by allowing the natural embrace of our mindfulness to come home to our body the way it is.

Often at the root of many kinds of suffering around body image are deeper needs for validation, acceptance, and love—we can give these to ourselves unconditionally by embracing our bodies as they are with our mindfulness: the most natural, connected, ever-present love there is.

We can practice a body scan by gently bringing our mindfulness to each part of our body, starting with our feet, and taking a few curious breaths with each part, exploring how it feels, and gradually welcoming and grounding our practice into our body.

We can start with our feet, and it may be helpful to move them around a little bit, or wiggle our toes, and take three to five breaths, kind of breathing into them, bringing mindfulness to them, being curious about how they actually feel.

Then, we can move up to the ankles, same thing, just taking a few breaths, connecting with any sensation we have there, maybe moving the ankle a bit.

We can continue at our own pace up the calves, shins, knees, thighs, and so on, just working our way up our body, one part at a time.

As we do, again, with each part, we can take three to five breaths, breathing into them, wiggling around a bit if it helps, welcoming them, being curious about how they actually feel.

I think of body scans a bit like massaging our body with our breath and our mindfulness. Very welcoming, loving, accepting. Any tension can be held and healed with the caring, warm, natural movement of our breathing.

And if we notice that we don't particularly feel that way, or have any manner of likes, dislikes, judgements, about our body, we can include those as well in our breath and our mindfulness. No need to believe them, noticing is enough. We don't have to be trapped in limiting or critical thoughts about ourselves—that's the power of meditation.

We can also stay curious. We've been in our body our whole lives, but how does each part actually feel? Is there space within it? Is it so solid? Or is it countless little parts moving together? Is there space within those? We don't need to get too analytical, but you get the idea, just very welcoming, friendly, and curious. Coming into and exploring our bodies.

The lower abdomen can be particularly grounding in terms of our spiritual energy and coming into harmony with our body in meditation, and when we get there, we may want to really take a few deep breaths way down into our lower belly and let them gently rest there for a moment or a few seconds before exhaling.

Sometimes people who have done different kinds of breath work or yoga ask if there are particular techniques in our style of meditation, and the one I just mentioned can definitely be something to try if we find it helpful. Breathe deep into the belly, like a bit below the navel, and letting the breath rest there for a few seconds before exhaling. It brings our energy down out of our conceptual minds and our heads, and into alignment with the sacred workings of our bodies.

Then we just continue our body scan up through each part of our torso. It's good to keep this relatively general, not too anatomical in terms of all the different organs and everything, and just really natural, curious, welcoming, three to five breaths with each part.

When we get to the top of the torso, we can scan down the arms, to the hands, and back up. Then gradually around our heads.

When we're finished, we can rest with our whole body breathing, allowing ourselves to feel our body breathing, and including everything we experience within our natural home.

Simply breathing as we do in meditation can be a pithy way of grounding our practice in our bodies, as can the walking meditation we do, but if we have more time, or find it helpful, we can practice a body scan like this at any point.

A body scan can also be helpful sometimes if we have trouble sleeping, though be sure to use it for that purpose intentionally lying down at night and not sitting up in our meditation:)

Feeling What We Feel

Mindfulness of feeling, strictly speaking, can be about including and connecting with the feeling quality that is inseparable from all our variety of experience. The infinitude of feelings can be roughly categorized as either pleasant, painful, or indifferent. They are part of every experience in life. Sometimes, in more technical presentations of the four foundations of mindfulness, quite a lot more is said about that, and teased all apart quite specifically. But here, I'd like to treat it more experientially and generally, in terms of embracing everything we feel in our practice.

Everything we feel is included in our practice. It can all, literally, be a foundation for our mindfulness, or a basis for our meditation. The more we can embrace and welcome it all, the more open our heart, and the stronger our practice and our lives can be. Feeling what we feel is a profound invitation to total acceptance and friendliness with ourselves. Because nothing is excluded, we become whole, and whole, we're strong.

This is one of the great paradigms of the meditative path. It's not about feeling a certain way, it's about *learning that we can feel all ways,* and learning that all feeling is an expression of life and an invitation to the fullness of being. We do this through total acceptance, friendliness, embrace, *allowing ourselves to simply feel what we feel, however that is, and welcoming it into our breathing.* And that's enough. We're enough.

This is as opposed to "here are my good spiritual feelings for my meditation practice, and then under the rug is all the stuff I'm ashamed of that really bothers me and isn't good enough for meditation." Rather, all of this is included in my meditation, I can feel it all, include it all, make peace with it all. This is the practice of shamatha.

All of our experience isn't just worthy of our practice—it is our practice. All, all, all feelings, are literally, a *foundation* for our mindfulness. An invitation to an unconditional presence, and an unconditional love. Caring mindfulness is the best friend we'll ever have, it's *always there*, even when we die. By feeling what we feel, we can always come home. Home to here and now, exactly as that is. We can do it, and we're enough.

In life, and in meditation, understandably, we often chase after what is pleasant, and avoid what is painful. In fact, we often define what is "good" or "bad," or even "success" or "failure" by what feels pleasant or painful. But pleasure and pain are both just a part of life. Sometimes things go our way, and sometimes they don't. We can feel both, and neither will last.

One of the best pieces of life advice I ever received was from my father back in Texas. He said "You know son, there's nothing wrong with feeling a little bit of pain for a little while."

He's right. One of the great revolutions of the spiritual path is that we can actually just feel pain, and leave it there. We don't have to entrap ourselves in "negative negativity," or the additional exponential layers of struggle, narratives, stories, rationalizations, judgements, self-critical or other-blaming dramas, and so on, that are often layered over what is at the root simply a painful experience. The sad part is, all of those make it worse, because they avoid the acceptance and loving contact with pain itself that allows us to truly heal. We can always give ourselves that.

Pleasure, too, will pass, and is not a true refuge. We can spend enormous amounts of time, energy, and money trying to chase it and make it last. Or, we can just feel it, enjoy it, and welcome it back into the dance of life.

In meditation, the more we can embrace all of what we feel, pleasant or painful, just the way it is, the more fully we can make peace with ourselves and rest in shamatha. We make peace by being willing to feel, otherwise we're fighting. We can't make peace with fighting, we make peace by feeling. And having made peace, we can truly rest.

Having accepted the feeling quality of our experience, we can also get curious about it. Where is it in our body? How does it actually feel somatically? Is there space within it? Can I breathe space into it? Does it last?

As I've described in earlier chapters, this can be an especially helpful way to work with any strong emotional energy which is stuck through either having been reinforced many times, or not felt and released fully at the time it was experienced.

We can drop any associated story lines or narratives, and get curious about the feeling tone of the raw emotional energy, finding it in our body, and exploring it, getting curious, breathing with it, mixing it with the space in the room, breathing space into it, holding it, loving it, caring for it, and allowing it to gradually open and release. Like massaging a knot in a muscle, but with our breathing, our curiosity, our mindfulness.

If we discover that as we do so, the energy begins to melt, resolve, and open up, this can be a way of practicing vipashyana with feelings or emotional energy—we're learning it's not actually solid. It's changing, has temporarily become stuck, and can return to being free and flowing.

Likewise, if we begin to understand that pleasant experiences also are fleeting, momentary, and never really solid, this can be a way of practicing vipashyana as well.

More and more, we may begin to cultivate and discover that we can actually feel everything just the way it is, include it in our breathing, remain present with it, and allow it to melt and open.

As we do, we may find that all feeling has at its heart the essence of connection, care, and life. All feeling has within it a longing away from suffering, an attempt to be happy. This is what we call compassion.

As our compassion is set free from the limitations of fixed notions of good and bad, happy and sad, pleasant and painful, we can discover a more real love. A more real connection, a more real embrace, something much more boundless, open, and free.

Compassion is heartfelt connection with others, with all of life, in a way that calls it home to the openness and freedom from which it came.

Mind and Wisdom

In talking about mindfulness of mind, I'd like to start by saying a little bit about what mind is. This may seem a little technical at first, but I promise, that won't last long, and it can help us understand how to free our minds.

When we say "mind," it's usually shorthand for "dualistic mind." *Dualistic mind* means "experiencing in terms of subject and object." Our thinking mind is one form of dualistic mind, and one that is easy to understand.

Say we're thinking about our mom. We have the subject, our thinking mind, and the object, the mental image of our mom. The subject, our thinking mind, may be imbued with all kinds of different emotions, memories, and so on, which then project the object, all kinds of various mental images of our mom that appear flavored by all of that, and together form a general sense of meaning, "mom," and all that entails.

Or said even more simply, when we're thinking, we're thinking *about something*. That's what we mean by "dualistic mind."

Dualistic mind can also perceive sensory experiences like the world around us, but in a way that feels separate from it, subject and object, I'm here and you're over there across the room and we're having a conversation. Or I'm watching TV. There's the "I'm," and then the "TV," and we're watching it.

Dualistic mind has to have an object. But it usually doesn't stop at just having an object, it usually fixates, clings onto, grasps at objects, and gets carried away with them into all kinds of thoughts, actions, patterns, and so on. Those start in our mind, but can be carried out into our speech and physical actions. These form cycles of action in our own lives, and also in relationships, societies...and all the world's a stage.

This is also why the thinking mind tends to form habitual patterns, or "reruns," or the same old narratives that keep playing themselves out in our minds, and then our lives. These can form cycles, for better or worse, but ultimately keep us trapped, going around in circles. In Buddhism, we talk about this as "karma," or "action." It stops when we stop.

The thinking mind has to think about something in order to exist. It's a little like the cartoon character who keeps running off of the cliff until they look down. Looking down is analogous to vipashyana, and I'll say more about that in the next chapter. It's how we free our minds.

What we call "wisdom," or "wisdom mind," on the other hand, does not have an object. It is not dualistic. It's intuitive, holistic, one with experience. And most importantly, it's very open, because it's not fixated on anything at all. Rather, it is one with all experience, one with space, brimming with insight, and overflowing with love and helpful actions.

Wisdom is definitely not trapped in habitual patterns, conceptual narratives, and karmic cycles. Those are from dualistic mind. Wisdom is wide open, free, nonconceptual. As well, wisdom knows what to do, and it acts skillfully and to benefit others. This is because wisdom truly understands, while dualistic mind can only ever really have so good an idea, accurate as those may be.

And at the same time, if dualistic mind is like ice, then wisdom is like water.

Dualistic mind is just a temporarily frozen form of wisdom, tangled and stuck by fixation, believing our thoughts, getting carried away, acting them out, getting locked into cycles.

This is why when we first notice and relax with thought, it vanishes into something much more open. Like clouds passing back into the sky, never separate.

We can gently introduce thoughts to the space they come from, and dissolve back into. Eventually, it's all a lot more seamless.

Wisdom is innate, and the more we set our minds free and embody our wisdom, the more happy, free, and skillful our lives will be because there's less and less holding us back. Life is more free flowing, and not trapped within limiting patterns and beliefs. Most importantly, it's imbued with compassion, and our actions can truly help others.

Just like ice and water, they're usually not all one way or another. Typically we're like a wintery mix, melting more and more as we practice.

Shamatha, at first, can be a way of taming the dualistic mind, and allowing it to rest with stability, clarity, and strength, on the object of the breathing and including everything we experience, as I've described. Learning we don't have to be trapped in our thoughts, and can make peace with ourselves.

Vipashyana can be a way of journeying from the dualistic mind to the wisdom mind, setting our minds free. The next chapter "Mixing Mind, Breath, and Space," will offer a very simple instruction for how to do that.

Shamatha and vipashyana returning to union means resting in innate wisdom itself, which becomes increasingly natural and effortless.

Mixing Mind, Breath, and Space

Now I'll describe a way of working with vipashyana that has a lot to do with setting the mind free into wisdom. We do this by mixing the mind with the breath, and out into space.

As you read in the previous chapter, the dualistic mind has to have an object, to which it usually gets very attached and caught up in activity. When it's free from the confines of an object, it's set free into its wisdom nature.

Our mind and our breath are also very intimately connected, and so now, we'll use all of these principles to our advantage in an incredibly natural, easy way.

We'll go ahead and give our minds an object: our outbreath.

We'll mix our minds completely with our outbreath, become our outbreath, mix anything we experience with our outbreath.

And we'll breathe right out into space.

With our gaze open, relaxed out a little farther than usual, just become our outbreath completely, mix our whole experience with our outbreath including any thoughts we're having, and breathe on out into space.

At first, it may be helpful to do this in an exaggerated way a few times, like feel the space around us in the room in every direction, and really breathe out fully and physically a few times all the way out. Then let it be natural.

Feeling the space all around us through our senses can help our mind start to open up or relax a little bit, and then breathe out fully into it, letting go.

Breathing out naturally, dissolving out, expanding out, letting go. Over, and over, and over again.

The inbreath will happen naturally, but we don't pay much attention to it. So this is not like how we've been practicing shamatha to this point, mixing our minds with the entire cycle of breathing, in and out. Now, in order to help open up into vipashyana, we're deliberately mixing with the outbreath and dissolving out with it.

As we breathe out, we may notice a "gap" in our conceptual minds, thoughts, or stories. We may have a little micro moment when everything stops. Even meditation, and no one really meditating. Yet very awake.

That can be a way of glimpsing vipashyana, and we just rest in that gap, over and over again, and very gradually, as shamatha and vipashyana return to one, we rest a bit longer at a time. We come home.

At first, it can be like a little break in the clouds, or a ray of sun shining through, and then back to the usual weather. That's OK, and the point is to keep dissolving out with the breath, and every little "gap" adds up.

This may go on for quite a while, as in dissolving out with the outbreath, occasionally noticing a gap, resting for a while, gradually longer. That's very good. That could be our practice for days, weeks, months, years.

As we continue to practice and trust that space more and more, we may long to connect with it more fully, understanding that it's true to form, the unfettered wisdom of everyone's nature, the sky beyond the clouds.

Some have realized it and can help us. Others haven't and can use help. But it's everyone, everyone, everyone's nature. It's life itself. Life beyond life and death.

With a heart filled with loving, longing, utter trust, we raise our gaze directly out to the horizon. We give ourselves over to space completely, expand out with confidence, open, and let go.

We let our minds be like the sky.

Confidence here is very important, really trusting the vastness of wisdom mind, expanding out, letting go.

At this point we're not intentionally meditating, nor applying any effort. Just very naturally resting with confidence. Letting buddha nature do the work.

As thoughts arise, we can gently introduce them to this space, the space they arose from, the space they are, the space they depart back into.

With enough confidence, thoughts can even be our friends, one as awareness unfolding, like sparks from the fire of wisdom.

If we need a little more structure, we can continue working with dissolving out with the outbreath.

If that feels redundant and like we can just rest, then just rest. It's fine to go back and forth.

Sacred World

Now our practice can include the whole world around us, and as our shamatha continues to open into vipashyana, and our mind into wisdom, we can see the world as it is: awake, sacred, free, and beautiful.

We can understand not our place in the world, but that we have always been one with the world, arising from it, and passing back into it.

We can act to help restore harmony. We can understand that mother earth herself is in a process of restoring harmony, even if that involves showing us the devastating results of our actions, and learning the hard way before we can eventually go forward more true-to-form many years down the road. But we'll get there. I promise.

On a much smaller scale, as our practice opens up into the world around us, we can engage with all manner of life situations in more helpful ways. Our world certainly needs that, whatever our sphere of influence.

And again, this happens a little bit at a time, and is a lifelong journey.

This final foundation of mindfulness, mindfulness of phenomenon, can be discussed in lots of different ways. It can literally include all objects of our minds, both within ourselves, and all around us. Here I'm going to emphasize the sensory world around us, and working with our sense perceptions in a wakeful way as a support or foundation for our practice.

Our whole world exists in interdependent relationship. The play of all the elements: earth, fire, water, wind, space, ourselves and others, societies and their creations, all exist in dynamic causality.

Every moment of life we experience is the play of infinite causes and conditions that have led to the present, and this present is open.

The freshness of meditation can allow us to meet this present moment the way it is, beyond preconceived ideas and karmic patterns, and to go forward in helpful ways.

Opening to our senses in practice can be both grounding and expansive in its own right, and can help facilitate this more life-long journey.

We can do this by raising our gaze farther out in front of us, even directly in front of us to the horizon. Looking out into the space in front of us.

As we do, we can allow ourselves to see what we see, hear what we hear, feel what we feel. Let the world meditate us. Trust our senses completely.

Our senses are expressions of wakefulness, and so is the living world around us. We can let it do the work, let it invite us home in every moment.

Let ourselves be held by the earth beneath us, and the world around us, letting it in through our senses, listening to every message, every moment.

With our breathing, we can continue mixing our mind with our outbreath, and dissolving out with it, letting go, over and over.

Trusting our senses, feeling the space around us, and dissolving our with our outbreath, all go hand in hand.

As we notice thought, noticing with curiosity is enough. Relax.

If at any point it feels redundant to work with the outbreath, just let go and rest with confidence, as we described before.

If we're spacing out or need more structure, work with the outbreath. If we become distracted or lost in thought, lower the gaze to more gently down in front of us, and continue in the same spirit of practice. If we get dull or drowsy, raise the gaze a little higher, and start fresh. Trust our intuition in making adjustments.

Little by little, we can open to our world as it is.

As we do, we become more and more free, and more and more able to help others, and to bring wisdom and compassion into life all around us.

Or rather, we merge with its natural flow, like a river coming home to the ocean.

About the Author

Gelong Loden Nyima has been a Buddhist monk for over fourteen years. His training was at Gampo Abbey (2009 - 2017), the monastery of Chögyam Trungpa Rinpoche and Pema Chödrön, where he completed an advanced cycle of traditional studies called shedra, practiced intensively for many years, and was empowered as a senior teacher. He designed and taught residential trainings for four years. He then lived at Drala Mountain Center in Colorado (2017 - 2023), where he served as Resident Teacher, designing and teaching many programs ranging from open audience meditation, to youth work, to Mahayana Buddhism. He's been blessed to receive teachings from many masters of the Nyingma and Kagyu lineages of Tibetan Buddhism, to have spent over three years in retreat, and to have supported thousands of people in their practice. He is a founding teacher of an ongoing Mahayana sangha called Bodhisattva Circle, and the author of Peace and Freedom, a pithy book on meditation. He now lives in his hometown of San Antonio, TX, where he will be offering events regionally and traveling to teach. His website is lodennyima.com